CHANGING CHINA

Opening Windows to the West

CHANGING CHINA

Opening Windows to the West

Text by Ron Wilson
Photos by Kevin Morris
Graphic Design by Steve Eames and Patrice Nelson

An OMF Book
Harold Shaw Publishers
Wheaton, Illinois

ISBN 0-87788-888-4

03 02 01 00 99 98 97
10 9 8 7 6 5 4 3 2 1

CONTENTS

Introduction: The New China / 7

China's Open Century / 10

On the Streets of China / 16

The New Consumers / 20

Glorious Wealth / 27

Farewell to Farms / 33

The Boom Towns / 38

Blighting the Land That Feeds Them / 42

The Gourmets / 47

Whatever Happened to the Family? / 52

The Coming Lost Generation / 58

The Leisure Class / 64

High-Tech Upheaval / 68

How the East Was Won / 70

Beyond Pedal Power / 74

The Resurrection of the Church / 81

The Coming of China / 89

THE NEW CHINA

When the Red armies drove the Nationalist troops out of China in 1949, a great sense of expectation gripped the land. "China has stood up," declared Mao Zedong. For the past century it had writhed under the harsh rule of the Qing dynasty and oppressive foreign powers, and Mao spoke defiantly. The country was at last united. The government began to eliminate the extremes of wealth and power and gave its attention to the plight of the peasants. All over China parents named their children "liberation" to celebrate the birth of the new China. Optimism prevailed.

In an unwittingly symbolic move, Mao Zedong took up residence inside a walled compound not far from the once-walled city of Beijing. China had been a nation of walls within walls, with the crowning achievement, the Great Wall in the north, as a monument to China's chronic fear of outsiders. Ironically, Mao had most of the city walls torn down to make way for roads and buildings. But he slowly built an invisible and nearly impenetrable wall around the country that for two-and-a-half decades kept the world from looking in and barred three-fourths of a billion citizens from getting out.

In the first few years of The People's Republic, foreign merchants, missionaries, diplomats and tourists fled as the new regime imposed tight control over every segment of life—the economy, the family, education, travel, the press, religion, etc. The central government regulated production, mandated quotas, distributed goods as needed, rationed food when necessary. Religious and dissenting

China has always borne a mystique for Westerners. The Great Wall, the Forbidden City and the Bamboo Curtain are symbols of China's centuries-old conviction that it is the Middle Kingdom, around which the world revolves.

political ideas and practices were suppressed. The nation lived in a time warp in which various five-year plans and campaigns and a so-called Great Leap Forward resulted in economic and cultural stagnation. The early years of idealism gave way to a Mao cult and to the Hundred Flowers campaign, which invited criticism and resulted in a madness that ended only with the death of Mao in 1976.

The new China began when Deng Xiaoping consolidated power two years later. He knew what he had to do. Slowly at first, he turned Marxist China toward a market economy and

"Market-Leninism," so-called, has transformed the cities. An entrepreneurial spirit prevails. With the influx from rural areas, Shanghai will reach 20 million by the turn of the century. The economic change is forcing a freer society with choices in leisure, education and religion not known for forty years.

opened the windows, firmly fastened for so long, to the West. Before long entrepreneurs appeared like bamboo sprouts in spring, first in the countryside as the commune system yielded to free enterprise, then in the cities. Foreign investors and experts—many of them Chinese from Hong Kong, Taiwan, the U.S., Canada, etc.—brought in new ideas along with their cash and their know-how. Rarely has a country changed as radically in such a short time as did China in this brief decade or two.

Soon, however, the pace of change grew beyond the power of government to control. More peasants than there were jobs flocked to the city to work in the new, privately owned industry. State enterprises, now in competition, trimmed their work forces, adding to the thousands swelling the cities and taxing the urban infrastructure. Inflation, corruption, crime, and a growing gap between rich and poor added to the woes of a central government which strained to keep the world's largest nation from coming unglued.

Still, the economic explosion opened the way for new ideas and gave millions the ability to choose where they will work or live or go to school or even what they will believe. Religious groups stirred and probed the limits of freedom. The press strained at its leash and found room to move around. Beijing tried to rein in the independent voices, but the heady atmosphere of even partial freedom had radical implications for the country and for the church.

The new China amazes visitors who managed to penetrate the walls during the time of Mao. Frenzied change now borders on chaos. In the cities, sportswear and business suits have replaced the ubiquitous drab blue Mao jackets. Coke and Colonel Sanders, Mickey Mouse and McDonald's grace the urban landscape, along with traffic jams and department stores. While 900 million peasants remain dirt poor, 200 million people have been freed from privation, and China watchers agree that the economic reform is irreversible.

This book is a quick glimpse through the newly opened windows at the world's oldest continual civilization in its present state of flux. Because the change is so visible, we have turned to photography to portray it. And because it touches so many aspects of daily life, we have had to choose only a few to write about. The result is a kind of photo album of a modern Marco Polo.

First, however, to make the contrast even more startling, we'll look back to a similar scene in the century past.

A growing number of Chinese now enjoy the latest creature comforts and a wide choice of consumer goods. Glittery department stores feature state-of-the-art electronics, Gucci styles, Rolex watches, and Christian Dior cosmetics. Some now talk about "The Great Mall of China."

9

CHINA'S OPEN CENTURY

A Saga of Merchants and Missionaries

A few years before Hudson Taylor stepped ashore at Shanghai in March 1854, China, under duress, had consented to allow foreigners to live in special enclaves in the major ports. For centuries she had resisted foreign penetration

to the extent that offenders were often summarily executed. But England and other Western nations, wanting tea and silk for trade, began to smuggle in opium to pay for them. China fought back, but the opium traders found support from their government and their gunboats. At one point, the emperor's commissioner wrote to Queen Victoria:

"So long as you do not take it yourselves but continue to make it and expect the people of China to buy it, you [are] careful of your own lives but careless of

A system of rivers and canals once allowed Western commerce and Christianity to penetrate deep into the heart of China. Today the waterways are clogged with barges laden with building materials, produce, and consumer goods.

other people, indifferent in your greed for gain to the harm you do to others. Such content is repugnant to human feeling and at variance with the Way of Heaven."

In what came to be known as the "unequal treaties," the Western powers forced China to accept the presence of foreigners and open major ports for trade. With the merchants leading the way, Hudson Taylor and other missionaries followed with little but the gospel on their minds and hearts. For decades

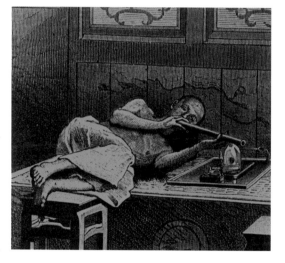

In the nineteenth century, opium smoking caused the death of thousands and enslaved many more. Missionaries joined responsible citizens in trying to ban the import of opium by Western traders, but all too often they were mistaken as perpetrators of the habit, poisoning the bodies and minds of the people.

they had worked at great risk in a few of the major coastal cities, but now, with their language skills, the traders sought them out as translators. Some missionaries, seeing the opportunities to reach into new areas, traveled on opium-laden ships, distributing Bibles and tracts and preaching in the ports. Others, like Taylor, eschewed the protection offered by the colonial powers, preferring to place themselves under Chinese laws.

Both missionaries and merchants looked longingly inland and across China's vast expanse. Christian historian A. J. Broomhall wrote:

"Disregard for the laws of Asian nations was inherent in the attitude of British merchants. In the treaty ports of China it was even more so. . . . The vogue was to test the constraints as far as possible. For any but the armed ships an element of real risk made treaty-stretching a fair sport."

In the years that followed, Hudson Taylor and others pushed into the interior at great peril and sometimes with disastrous results. Taylor had been inspired by great pioneers such as Robert Morrison and Charles Gutzlaff. His

passion for China was so great that he once wrote, "If I had a thousand pounds, China should have it. If I had a thousand lives, China should have them. No! Not China, but Christ." He was one of the first Protestant missionaries to adopt Chinese dress and wean himself of many Western habits, to the scorn of his compatriots in the treaty ports.

The way inland was finally smoothed by another treaty which legalized travel and residence in any part of the empire and immunized foreigners from Chinese laws. China's "open century" had begun, but it had been forced upon an ancient civilization that would not forget.

China did not bear its humiliation easily and outsiders trod carefully. In the Boxer Rebellion of 1900, for example, mobs killed hundreds of Westerners before a force from eight nations subdued the rebels. When the Manchu dynasty finally crumbled in 1911, Chinese patriots tried to establish a republic, but the country soon gave way to warlordism, Japanese imperialism, and, finally, civil war. The fighting ended in 1949 with Communist troops marching into Beijing carrying red banners and portraits of Mao Zedong.

Once more China closed its doors to Western trade and influence and expelled missionaries. China sided with the Soviet Union in the Cold War and

The literati, aware of their highly developed culture and of the glories of ancient China, looked on foreigners as barbarians. Wise missionaries found common ground for friendship with the literati by understanding Confucian principles and reading Chinese classics.

set about systematically to extinguish Christianity and all other religions in the People's Republic of China.

Today, once again, the engine of trade has generated an open door policy—but this time the impetus has come from inside. Twenty-five years or more of self-imposed isolation were marked by natural and social disorders, economic

depression, a decline in production, and a disillusioned population. Now this great nation, with the largest population and the oldest continuous civilization in the world, cautiously balances a policy of social and political control with a free market and a free flow of ideas. China has begun what all hope will be a second open century.

Aware of Chinese hostilities to foreigners and foreign ways, Hudson Taylor urged his mission members: "Let us in everything unsinful become Chinese, that by all means we may save some. Let us adopt their costume, acquire their language, study to imitate their habits, and approximate to their diet as far as health and constitution will allow. Let us live in their houses . . . and only so far modifying internal arrangements as attention to health and efficiency for work absolutely require."

ON THE STREETS OF CHINA

The open market in Yangzhou winds around a corner and runs beside a dried up canal leading to the Yangtze River. The massive, yellowish Yangtze and the Grand Canal meet here, and at the end of the dirt road you can look out over the powerful and unending flow that has witnessed 4,000 years or more of history.

An ancient dentist chair sits beside the road and a small table beside it holds a few drills and picks and tools of the dental trade. You can get a cavity filled here, or, if the tooth is too far gone, you can have it pulled. And while you wait, the owner of the next stall will mend your umbrella. This part of the market seems to specialize in repairs. A little way down the road, you can get new soles and heels, or you can have a spare key made while you wait.

Business is more brisk in the food section. Beside the large barrels of white and red rice, millet and sesame seeds, are a variety of foodstuffs including sea slugs, chicken feet, eels, and quail eggs.

For centuries much of urban life has been lived on the street in China, and the return of the open markets is a clear sign of departure from a socialist economy where private enterprise was not allowed. You can meet most daily needs on the street. Buy a bowl of noodles for 12 cents, 15 cents with egg. Fried rice or sticks of fried batter are available a few feet away. Or sit there under the umbrella and order a five-course meal. In the early seventies you could walk the streets of Shanghai or Beijing and see only the drab fronts of state-run commercial outlets that slammed their doors shut at 7:00 p.m.

Today in some cities life on the street begins at 8 or 9 in the evening in a sidewalk restaurant with a steaming plate of boiled dumplings or a bowl or fried noodles. Young men in jeans and T-shirts on gleaming new motor scooters

dart in and out of the crowds. Boom boxes wail a mix of pop, rock, and traditional Chinese music. An almost carnival-like atmosphere prevails.

It doesn't take much capital to go into business. Lay a piece of plastic by the side of the road and arrange whatever you have—a few combs or handmade wallets and belts, a cheap Walkman clone, a jackknife or a pot of flowers. On the street you can complete your wardrobe, right down to your underwear and wingtip shoes. Or you can pick up a new coffeepot or a plastic washbasin, a toothbrush

or a plaster bust of Mao Zedong, a bonsai tree or an antique tea service.

Of course, commerce is not all that happens on the streets. The sheer number of people going someplace, crowding the parks, preparing food, or simply having a cup of tea or smoking a pipe lends a sense of an open and industrious society. Life is shared with strangers. Elderly and young alike practice Tai Chi in

The rise of small industry in the towns and villages has filled the streets with those who once worked in the fields. Free markets have mushroomed. The collectives (group-owned businesses) have spawned a new mobility. Some of the most successful are couples, one of whom hangs on to a government job with its security while the other plunges into the sea of private business.

the parks. Mothers bathe their toddlers in a tub on the sidewalk. Modern young men wash their cars or tinker with their motorscooters.

Still, with the rise of the unemployed in the cities, it pays to be more cautious on the once-safe streets. Pickpockets and prostitutes frequent the crowds around the train stations, where throngs spill out into the open square on hot summer evenings. Black market money changers work the tourist areas, and an occasional card game erupts into a fistfight or worse. But mostly you see friendly smiles, a new openness spawned by the relaxing of economic controls, a sense of expectation brought on by the choices and opportunities.

Something has changed in China, and you can see it on the street. The sign as you enter Yangzhou, not far from the open market, catches the spirit of it: "Let the world see Yangzhou, and let Yangzhou see the world."

At the going rate of migration, by the year 2010 half of China's population will live in urban areas. In Shanghai and other large cities, many emigrants congregate in regional ghettos where they speak their local dialect.

THE NEW CONSUMERS

Nanjing Road, seen here at night, is the heart of Shanghai's upscale shopping district. When China first opened its door to the outside, consumers thought that anything from abroad was superior, and searched here for Western name brands. Now domestic brands are giving the imports a good run for their money.

A small sign in front of the Manhattan Plaza on Shanghai's busy Nanjing Road lists the shops inside. Like the directory in an office building of professionals, this one is unobtrusive, discreet. But the establishments themselves are anything but modest—Paris Parfumerie, Playland Boutique, Giovanni, Boutique Paradiso, Tintori Fashion, J's Wily Whip Cafe. They are the high end (well, almost) of China's new consumerism, enjoyed by a growing middle class, and found mostly in the large cities.

Once wealth became socially acceptable, buying followed. The flip side of production is consumption. So-called market socialism raised the standard of living for millions, and, suddenly, glitzy shopping malls, privately owned department stores and free markets sprang up to provide goods for the new consumer class. Where bicycles, watches and radios had been the material marks of success, Chinese consumers now covet VCRs, color TVs, washing machines, refrigerators, air conditioners, and full-size bathtubs. One survey showed that almost half of today's young people expect to equip their homes with a full range of appliances. (Second-hand TVs from the cities are now sent to the countryside for

resale.) Some three million new watches are sold each month. About 40 percent want to own a car and covet a bedroom for themselves.

Credit cards have found their way to China—more than eight million by the end of 1994—and the Bank of China would like to see 200 million by the year 2000. The major ad agencies—McCann Erickson, Ogilvy and Mather, J. Walter Thompson, to name a few—have set up shop in Beijing or Shanghai, and one watchdog firm predicts that Chinese firms will spend in the $17 billion range by the end of 1997. The Western manufacturers of toothpaste, pizza, peanut butter, computers, microwave ovens and Coca-Cola have discovered the vast new market of both consumers as well as low-cost labor. Coca-Cola announced plans to build 25 new bottling plants, and by the year 2000 three million Motorola pagers will be beeping across the land.

Who buys these imported luxuries— shoes at $300, cosmetics for $100 a jar, underwear at $100? Many young people, with highly subsidized housing and utilities or who are living with their parents, have large disposable incomes, and the frills and comforts from the West are status symbols. Still, more than 800 million Chinese work on the farm for less money a year than the cost of a television set.

21

Shopping, once characterized by few and shoddy products and nasty clerks, is now popular entertainment—shopping for the sake of shopping. A small group of super-rich have even entered a phase of conspicuous consumption, flaunting cellular phones, Rolex watches, and gold jewelry. Rolls Royce opened a distributorship in China,

Millions of credit cards now circulate, and ready cash from a bank machine is available, although still a novelty. The reality, however, is that the average urban household has little discretionary income, and the average rural household has almost none.

and shady characters sell powdered pedigreed lap dogs—illegal in most places—for sums in four figures. One restaurant in Shanghai reportedly offers a deluxe feast including tortoise, deer and wild crane cooked in Chinese herbs. The cost for the meal runs into thousands of dollars per table.

Without a history of shopping, the Chinese are developing their own consumer habits. The saying "never make a purchase until you've compared three shops" reflects the caution of people new at the game. They are brand conscious, usually leaving the manufacturer's tag showing on clothes and sunglasses. And they are moved by brand names that evoke powerful images—e.g. Prosperity or Treasure—or English names that sound like Chinese phrases with symbolic significance. With limited resources, they search the shelves carefully before they buy, and they expect to get complete product information when they ask.

Under the old system of state-run manufacturing, many Chinese products were shoddy—chipped tea mugs, lopsided rice bowls, fire prevention equipment that caused fires. Not too many years ago the minister of commerce bought a pair of shoes that fell apart the next day. He got his money back, but most Chinese were not so lucky. Now with the competition of private industry, state-run factories are having to install a higher level of quality control.

Most of China's new consumers do their shopping at the numerous free markets which clog the streets of almost every city. Referred to by some as "the great mall of China," they are generally long stretches of street stalls grouped by what they sell—meat, grain, birds, household goods, antiques. Second-hand books and Mao kitsch are just up the street from baked goods.

Cigarette lighters, shampoo, T-shirts, and underpants with a zipper change pocket come next. Follow your nose, and you'll come to mounds of fresh fish, followed by plastic water guns, costume jewelry, radios, and digital alarm clocks. The malls go into high gear in the evening when the factories and offices close, and a stroll down an avenue in Chengdu or Hangzhou or Xiamen can be a little like walking through a gigantic dimly lit, super-market

The economic reforms and the

According to one successful Chinese tycoon, eating out is a measure of economic growth. If McDonald's has its way, wrote forecaster John Naisbitt, 600 Golden Arches will rise over China by early in the twenty-first century, and Pepsi and Coke are fighting it out for number one.

Twenty years ago, young men wanted girls with muscles and strength enough for hard labor. Today they prefer the svelte look.

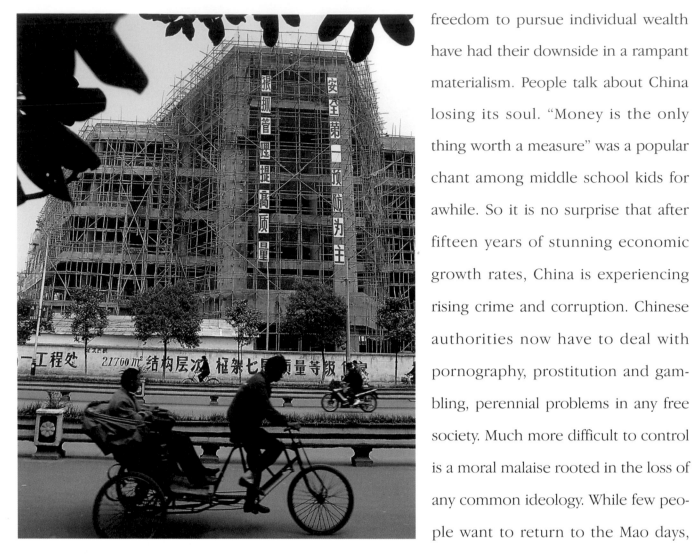

freedom to pursue individual wealth have had their downside in a rampant materialism. People talk about China losing its soul. "Money is the only thing worth a measure" was a popular chant among middle school kids for awhile. So it is no surprise that after fifteen years of stunning economic growth rates, China is experiencing rising crime and corruption. Chinese authorities now have to deal with pornography, prostitution and gambling, perennial problems in any free society. Much more difficult to control is a moral malaise rooted in the loss of any common ideology. While few people want to return to the Mao days,

Many Chinese cities seem like one big construction site. Foreign capital funds much of the building and architects compete to design office and living space for the next century.

older people have a certain nostalgia for the common sense of purpose they felt early in the revolution.

Still the economic revolution has raised 200 million or more Chinese from bare subsistence to a taste of leisure and a few discretionary yuan. And while China suffers some fallout from such rapid economic expansion—inflation, unemployment of workers in formerly state-owned factories, mass migration of job seekers—all agree that the dash toward a capitalistic society has just begun. Millions more happy consumers will soon join those now examining the lacquered furniture in the night market or slurping noodles in a fast food restaurant. Besides, when inflation reached 30 percent, the government imposed price controls to keep consumers happy.

For all the goods available, however, most consumers still have to take them home to crowded apartments which they share with an extended family. Mr. Hao is not unusual. In one rundown room he and wife and daughter share space with a refrigerator, a color TV, a telephone, a videocassette recorder, an air-conditioner, and a piano. The flux of immigrants to the city, plus the growth in population, have caused a chronic inner-city housing shortage. Apartments are state-assigned and highly subsidized (one reason Mr. Hao can afford the appliances), but they are very hard to get.

Now massive housing, much of it private, has turned the cities into a vast construction site. But the cost of these new low-rise apartments (if you have to ask, you can't afford them) puts them far out of the reach of the thousands of newcomers fresh from the farm. Workers can still count on a roof over their heads, but with the cost of center-city office space up to $4,000 a square yard in 1994, they'll find it at the edge of the burgeoning city. Of all the modern conveniences coveted by the new consumers, the most highly prized is a room of one's own.

Shamian Island in Guangzhou was once a foreign enclave on which Chinese were not allowed without permission. Today, many of the grand old buildings have been turned into badly needed housing. With the mass migration to the cities, housing will be a major problem for years to come.

GLORIOUS WEALTH

Ying Yiping, a former Beijing truck driver, began a company to restore historic buildings. Sunjin, once a political dissident, got so caught up in exporting clothes he stopped reading the newspapers. After working 25 years in a leather factory, Chen Zhong was laid off. So he set up a stall at the edge of Ritan Park in Beijing and began selling leather belts. Shaoshan, birthplace of Mao Zedong, is home to more than 2,000 private enterprises, many of them catering to the million or more tourists who pass through each year.

When Deng Xiaoping pronounced his now-famous, "To be rich is glorious," latent entrepreneurs, *getihu* they're called, sprouted on every corner. The rallying cry was *xia hai*, meaning "jump into the sea" or "go into business." The fever hit almost every area of life where two parties could exchange goods or services. Lawyers hung out their shingles; ad agencies and pollsters geared up to foster the glorious competition. Thousands quit their state jobs and began restaurants, beauty salons, tourist agencies and retail shops. Some with resources, skills and vision built factories; two brothers even began a private airline. Millionaires emerged, including a few old-style industrial barons, the type who fled the mainland in 1950 in fear of Marxist liberators but now squeeze

China is entranced with money, one journalist reported, and now buy pictures of Caishen, the god of wealth. Gone are the old drab Mao suits. These women in Zhenjiang look for colorful fabrics that catch the spirit of the new China.

long hard hours from their workers.

The Chinese economy, abetted by the large scale foreign investment which Deng encouraged, began to grow at a giddy pace. By the early nineties the annual growth edged to 10 percent or more. China began its own industrial revolution in an effort to catch up with the West and with its

Shanghai's Bund, so-called by Europeans, once housed the headquarters of many foreign enterprises. Now it holds many of the organizations that drive China's new entrepreneurialism as well as a few symbols of Western consumerism.

Asian neighbors. The nightly news featured shots of the leaders of blue-chip Western companies—-Chrysler, Motorola, IBM, Coca-Cola—getting the red-carpet treatment. (In contrast, in the mid-nineteenth century, Emperor Qianlong kept the first British trade delegation cooling their heels for two weeks before he would receive them.) Given the same economic freedom, experts predict the Chinese economy will grow outrageously for the next twenty years.

Chinese companies first began to issue stocks for sale in the late eighties, and in 1990, China's first national computerized stock exchange opened in Shanghai, setting off a new phase in Chinese economic life. Private banks were opened about the same time, but by then China was already well on its way to becoming the world's reigning economic miracle.

Some entrepreneurs, well-aware that on their own they would lose important perks such as subsidized housing, education and medical care, qualified the risk by becoming *yijia liangzhi,* meaning "one family, two systems," a play on *yiguo liangzhi*, "one country, two systems." In this arrangement, one spouse hangs on to a government job with its "iron rice bowl," while the other jumps into the sea of making money.

One of China's young fast-track managers, Zeng Wanhe, bills himself as a Confucian entrepreneur. Zeng oversees an odd kind of state/private arrange-

China has the world's fastest growing electric power industry, but still, the chronic shortage of energy threatens to slow the growth of the economy. The nuclear reactor to the left represents the country's hope to rid itself of pollution-spewing factories such as the one on its right.

Entrepreneurs with a little extra cash have looked at the stock market, a relatively new phenomenon in China, as a way to get rich quick. They've learned quickly, however, that the market is volatile and not completely predictable, and many have lost their new wealth.

ment in which the Beijing city government itself owns a department store conglomerate called Wangfujing that has expanded into warehousing, trucking, printing, shipping, and catering.

The Confucian side of his administration shows up in employee relations. An outgoing man who sings folksongs, he often socializes with the staff and mixes personnel development with hard-nosed business practices. Wangfujing employees can't count on the guarantee of a job that state employees had. Instead Zeng regularly lays off uneducated personnel, replacing them with better trained employees. The result? Steady growth and profits of $15 million in one recent year.

Other government entities—the army, for example, and various ministries—own their own side-line businesses with the profits going to the managers. Many are investing in Hong Kong and even in the U.S.

A billion Chinese racing for the disposable yuan has created a carnival atmosphere in some places. A hundred or more Chinese schoolchildren in white wigs, goatees, and string ties danced the Colonel Sanders Chicken Dance at the opening of a Kentucky Fried Chicken outlet in Shanghai. Local officials and KFC managers graced the event and predicted that the fast food franchise would spread its wings and hatch some 200 more outlets around the country. Inevitably, and to the great pleasure of Chinese officials, imitators arose. Across town, the Glory China Chicken Snack opened a similar emporium with "more Chinese characteristics" and cheaper meals.

While giant international corporations have poured billions of dollars into the Chinese economy, it is the small Chinese entrepreneur who illustrates the change and symbolizes the hope for the future. Bi Jiang is not the typical small businessman, but he does have the creativity and pluck that is changing the face of the market. Bi is a freelance writer who spends his evenings in his small room scribbling his prose late into the night. But in the morning he mounts his tricycle and sets out for office and factories, schools and army barracks to sell what he has written. With 17 books to his credit, he lives modestly and takes seriously his mother's dying words, "With your two hands do your own business, live your own way."

This privately owned electronics repair shop could not have functioned before "rich is good" became a popular slogan. Besides, the TVs and other household appliances which customers now leave to be fixed weren't available.

FAREWELL TO FARMS

The bright lights of Shanghai and the new prosperity in the major cities and special economic zones get most of the media attention; the focus is on changing China. In recent years tens of millions have escaped the austere drudgery of daily life and tasted a bit of Western consumerism. While this story of glitz and growth has been featured in the world's press, relatively little has been written about the 800 million peasants left to till the land.

In the early fifties, as one of its first major improvements, the new government took land from large landowners and gave some to everyone. Before long Mao took it back and began a system of communes. Twenty years later Deng Xiaoping turned once again to the countryside to begin the new economic readjustment. In the first of the so-called Four Modernizations, he broke up the communes and gave much of the land back to the farmers. Many were delighted. For the first time in a long time, they could work for themselves.

Under this system families contract to work a certain amount of land which they pay for in grain and cash. Once they've met that quota, they can grow anything else they like and sell it on the open market. With this kind of private incentive, agricultural output at first quadrupled, but leveled off at the end of the eighties.

Then in what some called a stroke of genius, Deng brought small industries to the rural areas and put millions of idle peasants to work. Many more, however, freed from the communes, fled to cities out of economic necessity. One writer estimated that some 15 million peasants each year abandoned the farms for the bright lights. And while many more have migrated than there are jobs available, every time one worker returns with a new suit and some flashy

An old Chinese story, "The Foolish Old Man," tells about the man and his sons who moved a mountain in front of their home, shovelful by shovelful. While family farming has returned and China is investing heavily in agricultural projects, millions of peasants still farm with hand tools and labor intensive methods.

costume jewelry, it inspires even more to seek their fortune in the city.

Unfortunately, as large as the country is, much of the land is arid and unproductive. Less than 10 percent is under cultivation. Millions of productive acres are being turned into industrial use, leaving less than enough to keep 800 million farmers busy. (This shortage of good earth is at least one of the reasons the government mandated cremation rather than burial for the dead. While tradition says that earth burial honors the dead, the planners considered it a tremendous waste of space.) Today, new residential housing blocks and huge factory complexes continue to encroach on China's limited arable land.

Ironically it was the peasants who made the Communist revolt possible, and while there are occasional protests in the countryside and some talk of a Peasants' Revolt, there seems to be little movement in that direction. For one thing, widespread hunger, as it existed in the late fifties and sixties has disappeared. You don't need a ticket to buy rice anymore. Zhou Enlai once said that China's greatest contribution to world peace was simply to feed its own people, but it has already begun to import grain. China feeds about four times as many people as the U.S. with only about two thirds of the crop land. That it can now feed its people reasonably well is, according to some experts, one of the major human accomplishments of the twentieth century.

While life has improved dramatically for many, the work day is still long and hard. Most peasants earn not much more than $100 a year. Disparity grows not only between city and rural dwellers but also in the countryside itself. The break-up of the commune has meant cuts in government subsidies such as food, health care and education, sending even more villagers looking for jobs in the city.

As part of an effort to reduce the proportion of people living in the countryside, urban planners have created hundreds of new rural townships and encouraged entrepreneurs, especially those who provide jobs for the ex-farmers. Thus former rural areas have turned urban without massive shifts in population.

Back in the city, many lament what one writer calls "countrification," that is uneducated and unsophisticated peasants crowding and littering the streets.

With not enough land to go around, China is accelerating research in experimental farming. This farmer in Jiangsu Province herds a flock of geese. A few years ago typical family fare consisted of rice and cabbage. Today more dine regularly on meat, fish and eggs.

Townies use strong language to disparage the country bumpkins and treat them like second-class citizens. Gangs organize orphans to beg on the streets and girls end up in brothels.

The migrants, however, are learning fast. The seventh century B.C. philosopher, Lao Tzu, wrote that wise officials would empty the minds of the masses, fill their bellies, weaken their wills, and strengthen their bones—a kind of Eastern version of the old Roman bread and circuses. In the new China, with its open windows and expanding economy, that kind of subjugation will be harder and harder for any government official to do.

These peasants (opposite page) in Sichuan, China's most populous province, carry their produce to market on the ubiquitous bicycle. Sichuan has led the way in creating small industrial towns in rural areas, thus stemming the flood to the cities and delivering workers to the new industries.

THE BOOM TOWNS

This span across the Huangpu River connects Shanghai with Pudong, the crown jewel in China's economic expansion. One year, New Year's visitors from the provinces refused to go home, shouting, "East, West, North, South—all can get rich in Pudong." China hopes to see these two river towns become the world's trade and financial center by the turn of the century.

In the early seventies, Shenzhen was a lazy fishing and farming village across a muddy creek just north of Hong Kong. Travelers from Hong Kong into the People's Republic got off the train at Lowu, carried their bags across an arched bridge into Shenzhen and boarded a Chinese train for the rest of the journey.

At the end of the decade, as China cracked a few windows to the West, this sleepy town was named one of four Special Economic Zones (SEZs), frontiers to experiment with a market-driven economy. Foreigners were allowed to invest, given tax breaks, and allowed to hire and fire workers. Managers in

Hong Kong moved factories to Shenzhen to harness the cheap labor. With foreign money, technology and expertise, these enclaves of capitalism became boom towns. By 1993 Shenzhen had some 9,000 Chinese-foreign joint ventures and had grown from a population of 30,000 to more than three million.

Success prompted the government to mark fourteen cities, all in coastal areas, for similar investment, and then to move the experiment inland. While the pursuit of profit has changed many smaller cities, two areas especially, Shenzhen and the Pudong New Area across the Huangpu River from Shanghai, have witnessed radical transformation from vast tracts of rice paddies to acres of sleek skyscrapers, broad boulevards, and gleaming high rises.

On top of the paved-over paddies of Shenzhen, hundreds of concrete factories

This bridge over one of Suzhou's many canals is slightly smaller than the one over the Huangpu, but it may be just as much a bridge to the future. Long known as one of China's most beautiful cities, Suzhou is now the site of a $20 billion industrial park, which, when finished well into the next century, will have more than a half million workers with factories from companies all over the world.

39

"The inhabitants of Suzhou make much silken cloth," wrote Marco Polo, and the industry has been the mainstay of the city's economy. But a fast-developing industrial park, modeled on Singapore's success and spearheaded by Singapore investors, should change all that.

spew out circuit boards, blouses, plastic chop sticks, and Disney dolls. Workers fresh from the provinces live nearby in fenced-in dormitories. Fast food restaurants and malls have sprouted among new apartments, glitzy hotels, and office towers, and the $60 million theme park, Window of the World, draws several million tourists a year.

While all is not as planned in Shenzhen—white collar crime is rampant—the flagship of the SEZs is thriving and is hailed as a model of modern China. Meanwhile, up the coast, the 200-square-mile Pudong New Area vies for the title of the nation's showcase of economic reform. Pudong already boasts China's highest edifice, the 468-meter TV and radio tower, and more than 3,000 foreign companies have staked out claims in the area. With big injections from transnationals such as Ford, IBM, Siemens, and Hitachi, investment in this hotbed of development has reached some $5 billion.

Like its southern rival, Pudong endures the dirt, noise and inconvenience of endless construction. The air is thick with dust and the boom of piledrivers. Workmen scramble over bamboo scaffolding, and bulldozers push piles of dirt and rocks around the emerging concrete structures.

Nor will it end soon. China plans to invest billions more in Pudong New Area, including funds for an airport that will eclipse the one in nearby Shanghai, and giving continued impetus to China's economic miracle.

In another type of urban development, Suzhou, 50 miles west of Shanghai, has been embraced as a joint venture with entrepreneurs in Singapore.

Suzhou has been around awhile—about 1,500 years—and already has a reputation for scenery and for beautiful women. But when the new residential, commercial, industrial and recreational areas are complete Suzhou will, according to its optimistic mayor, "merge Western civilization with Oriental style." Other planned communities, many on the outskirts of the major cities, are rising to meet the demand for industrial workers.

Back in the farm towns, employment agencies recruit employees and try to coordinate the movement of peasants to the city, but with only limited success. Some 10 million migrants have settled in Guangdong, and as many as one million sleep on the streets. Job seekers tax the infrastructure of most major cities. Still China sees the transition from farm to city as an opportunity, a necessary inconvenience in building the new China.

One wonders about the changes which these old men, looking out over the Pearl River in Guangzhou, have seen over the years. Radical as these changes may seem, they may be small compared to the expansion expected in the years ahead. The entire Pearl River Delta, from Guangzhou to Hong Kong, will meld into one large economic and industrial area, with major urban growth along the new expressway between the two cities.

BLIGHTING THE LAND THAT FEEDS THEM

"Men in smoke are like fish in dirty water."

The big red Chinese characters carrying this message were painted on the white clothes of Zhuo Xianbiao as he paraded through the towns and villages of Zhejiang Province. For years a lone voice crying, Zhuo ran from work each day to patrol the streets and shout at the citizens through a megaphone, warning them of the dangers of smoking. People called him crazy. Children followed him and laughed. Smoking is big business in China. About 300 million Chinese smoke and the tobacco tax is the government's largest single source of revenue. Recently, however, the government began a Non-Smoking and Health Association and appointed Zhuo an honorary adviser.

However, the environmental problem caused by smoking pales in comparison to the problem of industrial pollution. The same reforms which are turning China into a modern consumer society are wreaking monumental, and some say irreversible, damage to the environment. Several thousand development zones have been carved out of former rice paddies and farms, and coal-burning factories spew noxious fumes where rice or wheat once waved. The choking exhaust from thousands of new automobiles clogs the air, and some major cities have disappeared from satellite photographs, shrouded by a dense layer of smog. Pulmonary disease caused by sulfur dioxide is a leading cause of death. Beijing, long known for its clear blue skies, now smothers its treasures with gray smog from coal-burning factories and diesel and leaded-gas exhaust fumes.

To combat the pollution could mean slowing down the economic engine which is rushing down the tracks toward consumerism, but there are signs that the government is aware of the dilemma. In one recent five-year plan, for

Left: Tourists have thrown debris in a canal. Right: Garbage piled in the street. China's environmental problems will get worse before they get better. At the current level of consumption, experts predict the country will run out of trees by the end of the century.

example, it earmarked billions for the National Environmental Protection Agency. But while laws are passed on a national level, profit-hungry industrialists can easily persuade local officials to turn a blind eye to violations.

No popular trail-blazing environmental movement has yet gripped China, but some have awakened to the devastating impact which economic expansion is having on the land. One influential scholar formed the Friends of Nature, with modest goals to educate people about the need for conservation. Another group organized to protest the construction of a hydroelectric dam in the scenic Three Gorges region of the Yangtze River.

For all the injury being done, there is still a promising sign of concern for the beauty of the land and the safety of the people. Zhuo Xiangbiao's anti-smoking society reported some 80,000 members after 20 years. Zhuo even persuaded the officials of Changzhi City to bar smoking on one of its major streets.

In other cities the "litter police" sweep down on unsuspecting citizens who carelessly drop gum wrappers or cigarette butts. Vehicle emission standards have been stiffened, and some provinces are setting air quality requirements. A rapidly growing tourist industry has made it clear that pollution turns off visitors and is fast destroying some of China's greatest attractions.

Meanwhile, untreated waste water from the new industry pours into streams and rivers. In 1991 about 25 billion tons of industrial pollutants were dumped into the waterways. One traveler tells of seeing storm drains running through the city, reeking of solvents and "so thick with petrochemical wastes that they oozed rather than flowed." Styrofoam cups and packages, food wrappers, and other scourges of the new consumerism litter the roads and canals. Some 80 percent of the waterways are unsafe for swimming or fishing, and spectacular natural resources are being ravaged in the path of highways, factories and hydroelectric dams.

These blights on the land have resulted in random protests by ordinary citizens. In one province when a chemical company polluted the drinking water of a town downstream, the municipal authorities moved to halt production. When the plant's managers pulled political strings, the affected residents took to the streets. Hope now abides that such conflicts will help sober-minded government officials press forward with environmental conservation.

With several million new vehicles on the road each year, and much of its energy demand still met by burning coal, China is caught in an environmental dilemma. It is determined to build the greatest auto industry on earth, but vehicle emissions are already a major source of pollution and gray skies in the cities.

THE GOURMETS

"Governing a nation is much like cooking a small fish"
Lao Zi

Does Crispy Pigeon of Apricot Blossom appeal to you? How about Bird's Nest of the Southern Mountains? Or Beautiful Butterfly Greeting Guest? Such entrees from the menus of the better Chinese restaurants evidence not just China's traditional attention to cuisine, which goes back centuries before that of France, but a new affluence which makes this kind of dining possible. Eating out once required elaborate preparations and protocol. Today it's an ordinary experience for urbanites, and, in fact, carries such prestige and fills such a strong social need that more than half of consumer spending in China is for food.

With such a concern for food, it's not surprising that a major change in the social structure should affect what the Chinese put in their mouths. Food is a lens through which to see a society, and the changing patterns of eating reveal much about the new China.

The first change is simply the wide variety of choices now available and the increase in the nutritional intake of the average citizen. Gone are the long lines waiting for a few shriveled carrots or the ration tickets necessary to buy meat. In the urban areas, at least, the markets overflow with fruit and fresh vegetables, fish, duck and pork. Privately-owned street stalls feature pots of noodles, shish kebabs of pork, lamb or shrimp, steamed dumplings, hot soups, fresh pineapple, fried cakes, and deep-fried quail eggs.

For something completely different, however, urban residents, tired of the traditional, can patronize a Pizza Hut or one of scores of new fast food shops. McDonald's plans to have a hundred outlets in Beijing alone by 2003 and

Color, aroma and flavor are all important in Chinese cooking, making it an art as well as a necessity. Many rules surround the preparation and consumption of meals.

Timmy's, a local version of the newly popular fast food restaurants, is a popular lunch spot for Shanghai office workers. The rise of such outlets gives the lie to the old Chinese proverb that "even a clever wife can't cook without rice."

more than 600 across all of China. Baskin-Robbins scooped its competitors by forming a partnership with a military-run firm to sell ice cream. *The Economist* reported that Cadbury chocolate, Maxwell House coffee and treats from United Biscuit have won the hearts of the Chinese. The super-affluent can drop into the Louis XVI Deluxe Feast in Shanghai for a meal that will cost almost 20 times the annual income of the average Chinese. The restaurant caters to overseas Chinese businessmen.

Such abundance, while an extreme today, was unthinkable through the fifties, sixties and much of the seventies. Peasants were then exhorted to eat "Leap Forward Flour," which consisted of corncobs, corn silk, rice husks and wheat husks ground together. The flour didn't have much nutritional value, but it helped to fill the cavity. In fact the wide variety of items in the Chinese diet has come in part from the age-old threat of famine. With hunger at your doorstep, you learn quickly that a lot of things growing—or walking or flying or swimming—around you are edible. It is not unusual to find eel, tripe, squid, pigs' feet, grasshoppers, cicadas, and jellyfish all served at a banquet in a fine restaurant today.

Fried scorpion, tail and all, is considered a delicacy. Raised on scorpion farms, they're fed a diet of worms. Some compare the taste to fried pork rinds, but while the venom has been extracted for medicinal use, the pincers do tend to get stuck in the teeth. Other culinary delights not popular in the West include fox, baby pigeon feet, and fried buffalo marrow. The demand for chicken feet is so great that a vice president of the America's National Broiler

Council lamented, "We could sell a lot more but there are only seven billion chickens in the U.S., and each has only two feet."

Many Chinese provinces have a distinctive cuisine—Szechwan, Hunan, Guangdong (Canton)—but there are clear differences between the north and the south. Northerners grow and use more wheat while Southerners favor rice. Faced with a population that will expand by 300 million in the next 10 years, Chinese scientists are experimenting with genetically altered tomatoes and potatoes, and a new strain of super rice that will feed 500 million more mouths.

Today parents are beginning to face the problem of obesity in children. It is not uncommon among the new urban affluent to see fat little children who have been fed on a diet of Western foods including frozen foods and instant meals in a box. A survey found that about one-third of Beijing school children recognized the name "McDonald's," and another survey indicated that university students aren't eating right nor getting adequate exercise.

"Eating right" has now become important to many who are as conscious of nutrition as they are of taste and appearance. For most Chinese, however, the cost of the healthier "green food" is still beyond their means.

All this has helped to spawn a small but growing health food movement, "green cuisine." Major supermarkets have health food departments and the government has organized the China Green Food Development Center. Most of the consumers are university graduates and there is, no doubt, a little status involved. Green food is more expensive. A kilo of "no wash" rice might cost four times as much as the ordinary kind. In northwest China pork sales are down, but that probably reflects a revitalized practice of Islam there. Overall meat consumption has increased about 10 percent a year.

While fast food and the "green cuisine" gain popularity, traditional foods are still the mainstay of the Chinese diet. The difference is that people have plenty to eat and many more choices. Restaurants are booming and serve exotic delicacies such as fried scorpion and elephant ear fungus.

Health food or fast food, whichever, China's nutritional intake is fast approaching the world level, and dining, to which the Chinese have always attached great importance, will continue to change.

WHATEVER HAPPENED TO THE FAMILY?

The more the merrier, said Mao. Large families are the strength of China.

Not so, said a few wise men. Our population is growing too fast. How will we feed so many people? How will we educate them? Where will they find jobs? With nearly 25 percent of the world's people and only 7 percent of the arable land, the Chinese have had to make some tough decisions.

In 1966 China had about 600 million people. Ten years later they had added another 200 million. Meanwhile, Mao publicly humiliated a few leaders, including a university president who advocated family planning. Others he banished to the countryside or simply stuck in jail. Government officials disagreed over the value of population control; nevertheless they viewed each member as a unit of production and often broke up families. During the Cultural Revolution, husbands and wives often denounced each other as

China's population control program, so vital to its economic growth, has been weakened by resistance to change, the old Chinese desire to have as many male children as possible and the need for manpower. One researcher pointed out that the average annual increase in China's population in a recent thirty year period was equal to the total population of Canada.

"rightists." Parents were pulled from the family and sent off for re-education. Children were sent to day-care centers and often separated from parents for months at a time. Now, with economic reform, communes have been abolished, and parents have more choices for their children. But the changes have been hard on families.

Faced with the swelling population and the very real threat of more mouths than food and more workers than jobs, Deng's government at first tried education to keep families small. When that didn't work, it instituted a one-child-per-family policy and began to enforce strict birth control measures with heavy fines, job demotion, jail, and, if caught in time, abortion. Many pregnant women try hiding until after the baby is born. If caught, they're sent to abortion clinics. Others are brought in for sterilization.

Through constant pressure at all levels, the rate of population growth has slowed. Progress in agriculture has enabled China to feed its own. Food rationing, common during Mao's reign, is over. Still, the population has dou-

Don Emmerich

bled since the birth of the People's Republic in 1949 and has now passed one billion.

The one-child-per-family policy has had negative effects on family life, especially when coupled with the Chinese preference for male babies over female. Girls traditionally left the family at marriage, while boys stayed as an integral

As China's windows open wider, they are allowing in not just information about the world, but ways of looking at life that are radically different from those in the past. The exposure these children will have, in contrast to their parents, will widen the cultural gap that has already begun.

part of an informal social security system. Though the Mao government went a long way toward bringing equality to women, today many women, faced with the prospect of a female child, seek abortion. The prevalence of ultrasound scanning machines, which detect the sex of children before birth, has brought a degree of scientific assurance to the process and a drastic drop in the number of female babies. A news service reported that in one county ultrasound was used in 2,316 cases, resulting in the abortion of 1,006 female fetuses. Comments another newspaper, "Ultrasound is a wonderful thing for society, yet it also brings great tragedy."

The one-child-per-family policy means, obviously, that children have no siblings, and thus children in succeeding generations will have no uncles, no aunts and no cousins. Already people talk about a generation of "little emperors," pampered and selfish and demanding children who have not learned to share life with brothers and sisters.

It is an agonizing adjustment for people who have placed great value on having children. With only one child to dote on or to carry on the family name, parents push toddlers into pre-school education in private schools,

Children without brothers or sisters often receive undue attention and are called "little emperors." They are showered with everything their parents can afford and miss the values learned by children who share life with siblings.

often paying extraordinary sums to reserve a place for them in kindergarten. The real effects on the family and society will be seen when the generation of one-child families begins to look for mates and raise their own families.

Already, in fact, marriageable young men face a shortage of eligible women. The 1990 census showed 40 million more males than females, with nearly three men for every two women over fifteen. (The ratio grows greater as the

This family planning billboard in Chengdu indicates the government's concern about population growth. A hotline for marriage and family counseling handled 10,000 calls in its first four years, another indication of the stress faced by many Chinese couples.

age increases.) A government-sponsored matching service reports women are extremely happy because they can set high standards for a husband. Men on the other hand are taking more seriously an old Chinese proverb that says a man who marries a woman three years older has found a bar of gold. The situation is so critical the men now vie to appear on "We Meet Tonight," a television show in which the men put aside tradition and qualms and boldly state why they'd make a better mate than the next guy.

THE COMING LOST GENERATION

They strut through the malls in imported jeans and Nikes, peering skeptically at the world from behind dark glasses. Their T-shirts bear English words which often have no apparent meaning—*Boys, Elvis, Where We Are*. Or they gyrate in leather miniskirts and spike-heel shoes around the disco dance floors of upscale hotels. They sport gold jewelry, leather jackets, tight-fitting pants, silk ties, designer labels. Clothes—or, more precisely, fashion—make the younger generation in China today.

"We want style," one student put it. "We don't want to chase trends," another confessed, "but you know, clothing gets seen."

These are China's privileged, pampered but confused young people, a small but significant elite who answer the question, "What is the biggest worry in your life?" with "My income is too low." In a survey a few years before, "low income" had been ranked only fifth as a besetting problem for them. But the latest one revealed that money for tuition, getting a good job and other financial concerns dominated a lot of student thinking.

These are the same young people who pack concert halls to hear contemporary rock music, hard edged and ear splitting and now uniquely Chinese. At first the songs were sixties or seventies oldies from the West. Then Chinese musicians began to express the frustration of their own generation in transit. "Money floats in the air, we have no ideals," wails long-haired Cui Jian, classical trumpeter turned super rocker. And Dou Wie, one-time lead singer of a heavy metal band, sings about his personal nightmare: "I couldn't keep the family together ... Feeling desolate, I told myself I don't care." He Yon, sometimes called the Kurt Cobain of China, laments, "The world we live in is like a giant

Young people like these have absorbed Western values as well as technology, and they are the ones who are changing China. Individual subordination to the group, so-long enshrined as a spiritual value, is slowly giving way to individualism.

garbage dump/people are like maggots/we fight tooth and nail in this heap . . . some go on diets/some starve to death. . . ”

MTV has a 24-hour Mandarin-language channel that spreads the rock culture, and record producers from Taiwan and Hong Kong follow the top Chinese stars to clubs and concerts.

The music of the young reveals much about the cultural milieu. All Chinese young people, not just urban youth, float in a sea without tradition or values. Recent upheavals in society have left them with little attachment to the past. They've heard of the rampages of youth—of their parents, in fact—in the Cultural Revolution, but that's history, the past. The growing number exposed to Western media are becoming more like the young in other societies than like the older generation of Chinese. And one scholar warned, “The continuity

between generations, on which every society necessarily depends for its integrity and survival, has begun to fade." A clear example of this is the trend of Chinese young people toward focusing on themselves as individuals apart from their society, to place greater import on who *they* are than on the group. Some leaders warned that when the windows were opened, a few flies would come in. The Western notion that individuals have value appears to be one of them.

All this is normal, perhaps. With fewer guarantees in life, fewer subsidies of schooling, housing, and jobs, more choices in where they work or live, where they travel, what they buy or eat, young people begin to see themselves as the center of their world.

The great interest young people, especially students, have in religion should surprise no one. They are showing up in large numbers in Christian churches. In Henan at least half of the Christians are under 45. Westerners teaching English report an insatiable curiosity about Christianity as part of the students' search for truth. But then, Christianity is from the West, and as one young man told a reporter, "That's cool."

At the same time, university students are aware that they can choose their

Young people in the big cities descend on the clubs each weekend, where the beat is fast, the dance floor is crowded, and the atmosphere is electric. Shanghai, once dubbed the Paris of the East, is working hard to regain its reputation. Mandarin rock, much of it anti-establishment, gained a foothold in the nineties, along with Western music.

direction in life. They talk about the Red Way, the Black Way, the Yellow Way, and the Green Way. The Red Way is the way of the Communist Party, the way young people went for the past 40 years. It offers power and some security. The Black Way is the life of an intellectual. Get the PhD; teach and do research. You'll stay poor but you might contribute to the life of the nation and to society. The Yellow Way is the way of business. Making money! It's the new way, not available for many years but now officially approved. Finally, the Green Way is the way overseas. Leave it all behind. Study in the U.S. or some other Western country. Get a green card and make your life and fortune as one of the Chinese Diaspora.

"It is the younger and better educated who have separated themselves from the traditions of the past," commented one China watcher "They are enjoying experimenting with new lifestyles, and clearly these will be the easier sell for new products and services."

THE LEISURE CLASS

Young and old have shed their Mao jackets and caps and put on their dancing shoes. Western-style dancing, like this couple is doing at a lakeside pavilion, is popular. Pop and rock music came in with foreign capital. The old revolutionary music is rarely heard. Even Muzak has invaded the public space.

The road to Shaoshan from Changsha runs through the hills of Hunan Province, which are rich in the spring with the pink blossoms of milk vetch, red azaleas and yellow rape. It's a pastoral scene. Peasants still use hand machinery for planting rice. Little industry has penetrated this part of China, so the skies are clear, the countryside quiet. Except for the traffic.

A million or more tourists now travel this road each year to the birthplace of Mao Zedong. A new road carries them comfortably in air-conditioned tour buses to one of China's travel hot spots. They gape at the 14-room farmhouse where Mao lived, the barns and storehouses, the pool in front where Mao swam. They buy cold drinks and trinkets, take pictures, and climb back on the

buses, having paid homage to the man who is still known simply as "The Chairman."

Since the reforms began, the Chinese have hit the road. With a shortened work week—five days a week since 1995—and a few discretionary yuan in their jeans, a half billion of them each year are sailing down the Li River, wandering the gardens of Suzhou, paddling small boats

around West Lake in Hangzhou, gawking at shrines and monuments, and stuffing down Big Macs and fries. Entrepreneurs have developed attractions such as the Flying Dragon World Amusement Park (the first super amusement park in the world based on a snake theme) and the Window on the World, a theme park that has reproduced in miniature more than 100 famous world sites. Another three and a half million went abroad for business or pleasure in one recent year.

If knowledge is power, then those who predict the rise of China on the world scene may be right. Publishing has flourished under free enterprise. Books on business and technology, as well as romance novels and poetry are popular. Erotic literature is increasing, and magazines provide a needed market for advertisers.

In the old order, what leisure time the average citizen had was closely regulated. If it wasn't Chairman Mao Thought study classes or work in the fields, it was organized competition between work units. All that has changed. Dance halls were officially allowed in the early eighties and soon night clubs and Karaoke halls appeared. Books and magazines, once limited to production by the state, flooded the market. Educated folks began making money on the side by translating material, just about any material, from English. How-to books and pornography now share the book bins with Western classics and the biographies of the Beatles.

Nearly all urban households have TV but a Gallup survey in the mid-

With little leisure time during the Cultural Revolution, few people could travel or visit amusement parks such as this popular tourist spot in Shantou.

nineties revealed that more than anything else, the average Chinese wished for a color set. While State-run television still majors in soccer matches, documentaries, the Peking Opera and the like, cable operators have begun to bring Western programming. STAR-TV, owned by media baron Rupert Murdoch, began a movie channel. CNN is available. Chinese wives listen to Oprah Winfrey while they boil the noodles and munch on seafood-flavored, cheeseless Cheetos.

Talk radio has found a large audience both day and night, a million listeners on any given night in Shanghai alone. Listeners call in to complain about poor city services or noisy neighbors. Teenagers discuss sex and complain about parents. Parents worry about teenagers and complain about inflation. Talk show hosts encourage topics that people rarely discussed in public before.

With the liberalization, the arts have flourished. Novelists and playwrights, painters and musicians are pushing the perimeter of expression. Western productions such as Arthur Miller's *Death of a Salesman* and the award-winning *Music Man* have played in China. The rock music scene has exploded, and while it has begun to take on Chinese inflections, it has forced the windows to open even wider. Indeed, the new openness in the arts, a natural but bothersome adjunct to economic reform, has, perhaps, the greatest potential for breaking down the walls which once separated the Middle Kingdom from the rest of the world.

Also, unfortunately, the freedom has brought crime to the once-safe streets of Chinese cities. Thugs beat up the wife of the mayor of Shenzhen, who wrote to the government in Beijing that if the mayor can't even protect his wife, how can he protect the citizens of Shenzhen. Some conveniently blame the thousands of newly-arrived peasants. Others say that with the old guarantees gone, have-nots will take what they need from the haves. People now have to pay for what they once got free. One worker remembered when you could ride the bus for no charge. Today, if you don't have the change, you can't get on.

Organized sports were once the franchise of the State, but now students have more time for pickup games like this soccer match in Chengdu. Even that time is being preempted by the professionals on TV. Basketball has become the second most popular sport in China.

People have changed, some insist. "They've been hurt, undermined in their beliefs," one woman said. "It shows in the way they treat others. . . . They've become not just impolite but dishonest and untrustworthy. They no longer care how they behave, so they are rude, harsh, and always fighting."

Prostitution has grown under the new system. Truck drivers on major highways stop at "tea houses" when they see two or three young women sitting out front. Most of the women are farm girls who have given up the drudgery of the fields for the slavery of the brothel. Naturally, AIDS has followed on the heels of the new sexual indulgence. One province reported more than 2,000 cases of HIV positive patients, and some experts estimate China could have 260,000 carriers by 2000.

Of course TV has induced the greatest change in family life. Every Sunday night 30 million Chinese tune in to a soccer match between two Italian clubs 5,000 miles away. It's China's second most popular program after the news, and it reduces traffic to a trickle. One woman in Sichuan wrote, "You have saved my family life. Instead of playing cards with other men every Sunday night, my husband, my son, and I now watch in happy harmony this great game."

HIGH-TECH UPHEAVAL

Hospitals are scrambling for up-to-date technology, but equipment like this MRI machine is expensive. Private enterprise has reached into the health care field, giving the wealthy a choice besides state-owned hospitals.

Every school child knows that the Chinese invented gunpowder, paper, and the wheelbarrow. What most school children don't know is that Chinese scientists, long respected in fields such as math and physics, fell far behind their global colleagues in the years China was closed. Now, with new access to the West, they're redoubling their efforts to catch up.

About half of the country's scientists are engaged in research, but the pressure is on to link laboratory work to economic growth. The Chinese call this, "secure one end while letting the other end go," which means, simply, push some scientists and technicians into the marketplace, where they can turn the fruit of the laboratory into hard cash.

Not surprisingly, computers figure in plans to spur high-tech sales. In nine "silicon valleys" private high-tech companies are gathering, and many of them are hiring the hard-pressed computer scientists who are leaving for more lucrative jobs in Singapore or in the West. Meanwhile, surveys indicated more than a fourth of Chinese households would have their own computers by

1998, and the internet, with its attendant problems of information control, has taken root and is blossoming. Computer networks already link most of the universities and major research institutes, and some government agencies use videoconferencing. In Guangzhou a multimedia video network will offer entertainment and education to more than two million households. Of course, even with the 110 million telephone lines expected to be operating by the turn of the century, that leaves nine out of 10 Chinese without one. Not to be deterred, the government has encouraged wireless systems to meet the growing demand for communication services.

Without question the most ambitious technological feat, perhaps of this century, is the building of the Three Gorges Dam on the Yangtze River. The great Yangtze, celebrated by poets and singers, is famed for its spectacular beauty on one hand and its raging destructive habits on the other. Flooding has taken thousands of lives and wiped out many more acres of crops for several millennia. Planning began in the forties to stop up one of the most spectacular sections, to provide 15 times more electricity than any nuclear power station and to create the world's largest seaport in Chongqing. Environmentalists rage and wonder what will happen to the more than one million people displaced from the river valley, and the needed capital is slow in coming. But the dam builders keep digging to create what some believe will be the eighth wonder of the world.

China faces some formidable problems in its catch-up race. A young scientist entering the academic world earns only a bare bones salary. Thousands who went to the West for advanced study never returned, draining the country of some of its best brains. Disciplines such as high energy physics and space exploration are extremely expensive. So are nuclear power plants and high-tech weapons. China does extremely well, however, in solar research and in genetically improving crops, areas that require fewer funds for greater gains.

HOW THE EAST WAS WON

Conventional wisdom, reported the *South China Morning Post*, says that the Chinese don't go much for sweets, don't eat icy cold foods, and have difficulty digesting dairy products. Baskin-Robbins chucked conventional wisdom and opened an ice cream parlor in Beijing. It has been such a licking success that Chinese imitators are trying to freeze the American firm out of the market with lower prices.

While it's popular in some circles to defame America, Chinese consumers are voting with their yuan for more of everything from the West—refrigerators, air conditioners, cosmetics, fashions. Even retail practices such as, "the customer is always right," have taken root. "We're in business for service and in service for business," the manager of a state-owned corporation told a reporter. In the first flush of consumerism, shoppers thought if it was made abroad it was better.

American and European television and films have put their stamp on Chinese lifestyles. Hollywood stars adorn wall calendars. Everyone wants to learn English. Students attach themselves to tourists and business people so they can practice, asking endless questions about life outside China. Millions tune in to the BBC or the Voice of America. Scholars explore Christianity, seen, ironically, as a Western religion.

In a desperate competitive drive, market researchers have invaded urban Chinese homes to study buying behavior. Western firms from Bayer to Nescafe to Neilsen want to understand the attitudes and lifestyles of the new consumer in the People's Republic.

Unfortunately, the media serve up a mixed view of America. Movies from Hong Kong and some from the U.S. depict a crime-ridden, poverty-stricken U.S. on the rocks. (Some five billion movie tickets were sold in 1995.) One Jackie Chan Kung-fu movie pictured motorcycle gangs terrorizing Chinese convenience store owners in New York. Urbanites see well-dressed tourists nonchalantly flash credit cards and traveler's checks as they dart in and out of

A few of the new rich may drop several hundred dollars or more for a dress or suit, but most young people in the cities scrimp for a $20 pair of jeans or a new top. Clothing is a way of expressing individualism—not always a popular idea in China—and Chinese fashion designers have begun to add Chinese flair to Western clothes.

the sanctuary of three- and four-star hotels. One survey of 14- to 34-year olds showed more than half thought of America as the "least friendly to China." Still, surveys show that America is the country most Chinese would like to visit.

English words and Western images pop up in advertising, on newsstands, in stores, on television. Imitations and knockoffs of Western products show up in such diverse areas as fashion shows and biker magazines, hotlines and pampered pets, Coca-Cola and novels. Given a choice of local soft drinks or Coke, sales show most Chinese will take the Western drink. Coke sales increased by 76 percent in 1994 and some legislators called for laws to protect national products. By mid-1996, KFC had 75 outlets in 28 cities and McDonald's had 63.

Kitsch accounts for much of the imagery. "Beauty" calendars sport Western film stars or scenes of the Grand Canyon or the coast of Maine. Greeting cards and postcards picture Western families or landscapes.

Much of this stems from plain old curiosity. Isolated for so long, they now want to learn and experience the outside world. The years of ridicule of European and American ways have given way to a voracious appetite for all things Western especially among young people.

Opening the windows, has, no doubt, wreaked havoc with the historical Chinese sense of superiority over foreign ways and provoked a national identity crisis. Not far beneath the surface lies the humiliation evoked by several

centuries of economic and military invasion. Meanwhile traditional morality, religion, education, family life, and economics have all been challenged. And with easy access to information and the ability to travel, East and West are now integrated to a degree unknown before.

BEYOND PEDAL POWER

Mr. Kang, a bus driver in Shenzhen, was in such a hurry he opened the door before the bus had come to a full stop. When passengers jumped off, a policeman jumped on and gave Mr. Kang a ticket. His punishment: a fine of about $13 U.S., plus a day standing on a street corner waving a white flag that said, "Don't break the law." Jaywalkers in this boom town must wear a scarlet arm band and go out and catch three more jay walkers.

In spite of the invasion of four-wheel vehicles, the standard-issue black bicycle is still king in China, and 30 manufacturers pump millions more into the market each year. Bicycles are used to get to work or take the children to school, to carry a load of furniture or a squealing pig, even by bank robbers for escape.

Traffic problems of the four-wheeled kind are new to China. When economic reforms began in 1979, only about 150,000 cars ran around the country. By 1995, three or four million vehicles clogged the roads, and this number was expected to triple, at least, by the year 2000. The land of 460 million bicycles—the Bicycle Kingdom—is fast becoming an automobile culture, although sales of cycles have dipped only slightly.

Formerly, phalanxes of bicycles glided through the cities weaving in and out among themselves with unwritten rules of the road. They still share the road with a few horses, mules, and tractors, and not a few motorbikes and bicycles

Corporate executives as well as delivery men ride bicycles, but they share the road with a few horses and mules, tractors and motorbikes. No one pays attention to white or yellow lines, nor bicycle bells, which you can't hear anyhow when the horns begin to blow.

bearing enormous loads. But now bicyclers breathe the fire and fumes of the growing number of buses, trucks, taxis, and that ultimate consumer status symbol, the private sedan. Now the world's major car companies are racing to see who can build a low-cost car to fit the Chinese family's budget. This may still be a few years away, but with the government set to offer incentives to car buyers, the so-called "people's car" may run by the turn of the century.

Rush hour in the major cities lasts all day, except for about a two-hour break at noon. Beijing routinely denies licenses to motorbikes in an effort to limit the number on the road. In Shanghai, gridlock often paralyzes traffic. The streets are too narrow for the load, and widening them would bring on other problems such as the destruction of tens of thousands of badly needed housing units. In a show of egalitarianism, the government auctioned off some of its luxury limousines, and officials who once enjoyed the back seats of Mercedes, Cadillacs and BMWs now ride in Chinese-built cars.

Owning a driver's license has become a status symbol. As one young man put it, "It's a requirement for being a modern person." So he and millions of

The major Chinese cities at rush hour are pure chaos. Even the dauntless Chinese cyclist would think twice about entering this melee in Shanghai. Beijing and Shanghai now have subway systems. Guangzhou is building one, and other medium-sized cities are making plans for modern mass transit.

others have flocked to driving schools. Having learned how to speak English, then run a computer, one unemployed secretary expressed it, "It's a kind of fashion. I don't have a car, but everyone is learning how to do it."

Market reforms and population shifts have taxed China's entire transporta-

Travelers from the provinces camped in the square outside the Guangzhou railway station are a daily sight, not just on holidays. China is investing heavily in railways and roads, airports and harbors to alleviate its transportation crisis.

tion system. During a recent Spring Festival, 150 million people headed home to celebrate. Travelers camped outside train and bus stations for days to secure tickets. The airlines put on 3,500 extra flights. The government has made transportation a top priority. According to futurologist John Naisbitt, the government plans to spend three billion dollars for a 1,500-mile railroad between Beijing and Hong Kong and six billion dollars on roads, a port, and telecom links for Shanghai's new Pudong district.

Air travel is taking off quickly. More than 10 million passengers each year pass through the Beijing airport, originally built to process five million. The new airport under construction will accommodate 30 million. Boeing estimates China to be the fastest growing market for new aircraft, and travelers who once told wild tales of kids in the cockpit and luggage piled in the aisles

China's overtaxed airline industry endured a lot of criticism and some pointed jests in the public's concern for safety. Now the U.S. Federal Aviation Authority has helped its Chinese counterpart establish new maintenance regulations, and Western firms have set up pilot training programs which have given the country one of the best records in the industry.

now fly Chinese air lines with little concern for their safety.

The road from Guangzhou to Shenzhen, which borders Hong Kong, perhaps one of the busiest because it links two of the most prosperous special economic zones, once took four to five hours to traverse. Fatalities were too common to count, and the potholes turned new vehicles into beaters after several runs. Now a six-lane, 100-mile super toll road conveys vehicles comfortably from one city to the other. Other major road openings include a 340-kilometer Chengdu-to-Chongqing expressway.

Meanwhile, travelers in China should find the service improved and the waiting more pleasant because of new regulations issued to employees. Not known for their respect for paying customers, transportation workers are now forbidden to utter phrases such as: *"Don't you see I'm busy!"* or *"Go ask someone else,"* or *"Hurry up and pay."* Upon pain of dismissal, they are urged to smile and say *please* and *thank you.*

THE RESURRECTION OF THE CHURCH

The economic reforms of the eighties and nineties, intended to improve the material lot of the people, have also, unwittingly, helped the growth of the church. The case of a woman who opened a small food shop in an eastern city (we'll call her "Wu"), points this out.

Millions of peasants from Sichuan or Yunnan or Gansu or other inland provinces have abandoned their villages looking for work in the cities, and some of them frequent Wu's shop. She can easily tell them by their accents, and while many big city residents look on the newcomers with disdain, Wu often asks them if they know Jesus and invites them to church. Two men from a western province accepted her invitation to a church meeting. When one had an accident and the Christians came to his aid, both men were so moved that they became Christians. Months later when they returned to their province, they brought the gospel of Christ to their home town where it began to flourish. It was, of course, the reforms that made it possible for Wu to open a shop and for the men to travel freely from one city to the other.

Many church buildings were turned into community centers in the early years of the revolution. Others were boarded up or vandalized. As soon as they were returned, they filled up with the faithful, as well as a new generation of seekers.

One Chinese pastor calls this "the spring of Christianity" because more people are going to church than ever before. By all standards the church is alive and may be growing faster with limited freedom than it did when missionaries tramped up and down the land in the early part of the century.

When Mao marched into Beijing in 1949, the missionaries moved out

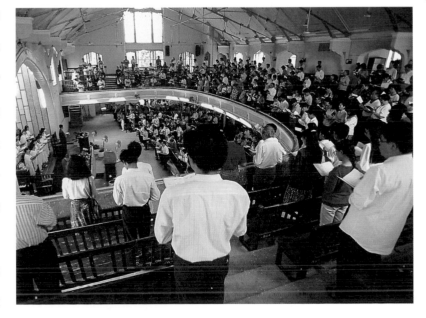

under great pressure and largely for the sake of Chinese Christians who would fare better without the association of friends from the West. Church buildings were closed and often turned over to local authorities, who used them for theaters or schools or even warehouses. Pastors were sent to the fields for "re-education." The church moved underground; many thought it had even been extinguished. A Hong Kong newspaper headlined a story, "Christianity in Shanghai Comes to an End."

When the reforms began in the late seventies, China relaxed its policies on religion and began to return church buildings to the faithful. A church building in Shanghai, which served as a detention center for criminals during the Cultural Revolution, was reopened as a church and now has four services every Sunday with about 3,000 in attendance each week.

As Christians returned to public awareness, both the official, government-sanctioned churches and the underground churches grew rapidly. At first mostly older people attended, but now young people pack out many churches. Intellectuals, by their nature a skeptical segment of the population, have increasingly shown interest in the gospel. In 1989 one visitor reported Bible studies on the campus of Beijing University. One night a week a house church in Guangzhou is crammed with several hundred university-age young people who closely follow an hour-and-a-half-long Bible study and sermon. A *New*

Churches such as the ones on these two pages attract both the faithful and the curious on Sunday morning. Others, looking for something to believe, are exploring various religious movements or following whatever healer or outright quack comes along. All agree that sects and heresies are on the increase.

York Times correspondent reported that "the fundamental attraction of Christianity is that it offers young people a spiritual anchor at a time when they have little else to believe in." One Westerner summarized a year teaching English in a Chinese university this way: "I have made *hundreds* of new friends on my campus and at 20 other campuses, where I lectured and visited. At one school in a neighboring city I made a speech to 2,000 students. Of my dozens of close friends, I believe that 34 are in one of the following categories: (1) they have made a decision to receive Christ as the Savior, or (2) they are praying about it, or (3) they are reading the Bible and going to church services. Fourteen of those are telling others about the Lord."

Conditions vary from one part of the country to another, but a former diplomat who has returned to China many times in recent years wrote about his findings: "I have visited well-educated pastors and believers in Beijing and Shanghai, and illiterate tribespeople in Guizhou. From registered home-meetings in remote Xinjiang to thriving congregations on the Fujian seaboard, nearly everywhere I have been impressed by the crowds of Christians and inquirers, and the depth of Christian devotion and spirituality." All observers agree that Bibles are hot items but are in short supply.

A few city congregations, touched by the economic revolution, have built modern buildings from the profits and the tithes of parishioners. One such church in Wenzhou sports 20-foot-high wooden doors that lead into a 2,500-seat auditorium. A 1,500-pound forged bell calls the population to worship.

Many explanations have been offered for what has been called "the resurrection of the Chinese church," and which has affected both Protestants and Catholics. The old ideals have collapsed, and there is a moral vacuum, some say. A soul-less materialism has grasped the country, and this is a reaction to it,

The 28 movements of Qigong, some of which resemble Tai Chi, have become a religion for many. Qigong masters gather large followings and many claim powers of magic and healing.

say others. More than a few point to the true signs of revival.

Interest in Buddhism, in the traditional Chinese gods (such as Caishen, the god of wealth), and in various new sects is also on the rise. A representative of the Chinese Buddhist Association put it this way, "Once people acquire wealth, they realize they are spiritually deprived. Then they seek religion."

The revival of interest in Mao has taken on a bizarre, cult-like

dimension. Likenesses of the Chairman grace calendars, knickknacks, pins, comic books, pencils, dinner plates, jewelry, and all kinds of kitsch. The mania for Mao memorabilia has a pop-art atmosphere but the underlying seriousness of a superstition.

One story, apocryphal perhaps, but telling, reported on a two-car collision. Someone noticed that the driver of the car that had a picture of Mao hanging from the rear-view mirror came out okay, but not so the other driver. Supposedly that spurred sales of the pictures which dangle from rear-view mirrors all over the country.

Confucius, too, is having a revival. Rejected earlier in the century by intellectuals and scorned by Communists, Confucian ethics are now seen as spiritual grounding for an increasingly materialistic society. Confucius taught that

Many young people and academics, free to examine new ideas, are looking at Christianity and studying the Bible. While some Bibles are available, university students clamor for the Scriptures in English, which are especially difficult to get.

"A people that considers material benefits higher than everything will have no hope," said President Jiang Zemin. He added, "We must cling to a spiritual pillar." Clearly, religion, with Chinese characters, is making a comeback.

individuals should put the welfare of the nation and the sanctity of the family before themselves. "Self-cultivation," the art of examining oneself for shortcomings and finding merit in others, is the foundation of Confucian morality and is now taught in schools.

Millions of Chinese are re-examining Qigong, a series of exercises much like Tai Chi. While it supposedly has healing qualities and is touted as therapy, it was created by the founder of Zen Buddhism and many consider it to be a religion.

Christianity, a foreign religion, bears the stigma which the Chinese traditionally attach to outside ideas. The fact is, however, that as the windows and doors to the West continue to let in money, goods, and ideas, interest in Christianity has grown. Along with Western movies and music, styles and technology, Christianity, which, ironically, grew first in the Middle East, is attracting the attention of a curious and spiritually famished generation of Chinese. A 34-year-old travel agent at a Catholic church put it this way, "Maybe I'm not a believer, but this is Western culture, and I want to learn more about it. This is a very famous religion."

THE COMING OF CHINA

China has opened its doors and windows, tightly closed for so long, and re-engaged the world, economically, politically, and socially. And as Asia itself takes on new significance in the world, China, more than simply being the largest of nations, brings a dynamic to the scene that makes it truly a leader in the modern reshaping of life on our planet. John Naisbitt puts it succinctly: "The Chinese are coming." It is more accurate, perhaps, to say that China is here.

The West is only slowly taking note of this shift, and its response is more often marked by curiosity than by serious consideration of what this means. But as 2000 A.D.—the Year of the Dragon—approaches, governments, the media, commerce, the church, and all major institutions will be forced to restructure their priorities and their lives to accommodate the "Dragon Century" to follow.

For all its changes—fast food and personal computers, discos and talk radio, expressways and private enterprise-—China is of the East, and the Chinese approach reality quite differently than people from the West. Westerners imbued with a rugged individualism do not always appreciate the Chinese attempt to find harmony with the world as a whole.

As East and West are inexorably drawn together, we in the West, will need to go deeper than the images on these pages. We will need to listen seriously, to study, to grasp the breadth of the history and the complexity of the culture and the language. We will need to strip the gospel of Western dress and marvel

at the blossoming of the Chinese church. We will need to approach this great land and its people, in the midst of a grand renaissance, with understanding and with the love that the apostle Paul called "a more excellent way." And we need to do it soon!

May the love of God descend on this great land and its people in the new Open Century that lies before it.

CREDITS

Material for the text of this book came from both first-hand observation and from secondary sources. The writer drew heavily on reports in newspapers and magazines, including *The China Daily*, published by the People's Republic of China. The following books were especially helpful in understanding the changes in China today:

China Pop, Jianying Zha, The New Press, 1995

China Today, Donald and Constance Shanor, St. Martin's Press, 1995

China Wakes, Nicholas D. Kristoff and Sheryl Wudunn, Times Books, 1994

Discos and Democracy, Orville Schell, Anchor Books, 1988

The Dragon's Brood, David Rice, Harper Collins, 1992

Fodor's China, Fodor's Travel Publications, 1992

Hudson Taylor & China's Open Century, A. J. Broomhall, Hodder & Stoughton, 1989

Mandate of Heaven, Orville Schell, Simon & Shuster, 1994

Resurrection of the Chinese Church, Tony Lambert, Harold Shaw Publishers/OMF Books, 1994

*This book was created by a team of
men and women who share in a
small way the love which Hudson
Taylor had for the people of China.
They were responsible for the idea,
management, writing, photography,
design, and production of the book,
and they include David Dougherty,
Steve Eames, Mark Ellis, Stu Imbach,
Kevin Morris, Patrice Nelson,
James H. Taylor III, and Ron Wilson.*